4/3

THE STORY OF LIFE

Clare Hibbert

E **Enslow Publishing**
101 W. 23rd Street
Suite 240
New York, NY 10011
USA
enslow.com

Published in 2019 by Enslow Publishing, LLC.
101 W. 23rd Street, Suite 240, New York, NY 10011

Cataloging-in-Publication Data

Names: Hibbert, Clare.
Title: The story of life / Clare Hibbert.
Description: New York : Enslow Publishing, 2019. | Series: Science explorers | Includes glossary and index.
Identifiers: ISBN 9781978506732 (pbk.) | ISBN 9781978506466 (library bound) | ISBN 9781978506787 (6pack)
| ISBN 9781978506534 (ebook)
Subjects: LCSH: Life (Biology)—Juvenile literature. | Life—Origin—Juvenile literature. | Evolution—Juvenile literature.
| Genetics—Juvenile literature.
Classification: LCC QH309.2 H625 2019 | DDC 576—dc23

Printed in the United States of America

To Our Readers: We have done our best to make sure all website addresses in this book were active and appropriate when we went to press. However, the author and the publisher have no control over and assume no liability for the material available on those websites or on any websites they may link to. Any comments or suggestions can be sent by email to customerservice@enslow.com.

Photo Credits:
Every attempt has been made to clear copyright. Should there be any inadvertent omission, please apply to the publisher for rectification.
Key: b-bottom, t-top, c-center, l-left, r-right
Alamy: 6–7 (David Fleetham); Arcturus Publishing Ltd: 24br & 31br (Stefano Azzalin); FLPA: 20–21 (Frans Lanting); NOAA Photo Library: 18cr & 27tr (Lost City 2005 Expedition/OAR/OER); Science Photo Library: 4–5 (Photo Insolite Realite), 10tr & 31bl (Kateryna Kon), 20c (Smetek), 24–25; Shutterstock: cover (main) & 14trbl (hillmanchaiyaphum), cover tr & 15tlb (Romeo Andrei Cana), cover bc & 15tr (Zety Akhzar), cover bl & 15tc (Victor Tyakht), cover tl & 15br & 30br (Laura Dinraths), cover cr & 12br (Molly NZ), 4tr (adriaticfoto), 4c (Neal Pritchard Media), 4br (YC_Chee), 5tr (adike), 5br (NASA Images), 6cr & 32br (Lightspring), 6bc (Susan Schmitz), 8–9 (hamdee), 8l (Calmara), 9cr (koya979), 10–11 (ranjith ravindran), 10c (Designua), 11cr (Designua), 12–13 (Brannon_Naito), 12cr (Sakura), 13bl (BlueRingMedia), 14tr (tcareob72), 14trbr (Popova Tetiana), 14ct, 14ctr (schankz), 14c (Andrey Armyagov), 14cbr (F Neidl), 14cb (Gerald Robert Fischer), 14bl (dangdumrong), 14br (Jolanta Wojcicka), 15ct (Rich Carey), 15ctr (Salparadis), 15cb (scubaluna), 15bc (Rich Carey), 16–17 (sebi_2569), 16cl (Bildagentur Zoonar GmbH), 16bl (Christos Georghiou), 17cr (yougoigo), 18–19 (Miami2you), 19tl (Budimir Jevtic), 19br (Sebastian Kaulitzki), 21bl (MatiasDelCarmine), 22–23 (Hedrus), 22bl (Esteban De Armas), 23tl (Panda Vector), 24cl (Tatsiana Salayuova), 25bl (kalen), 26tr (Warpaint), 26tl (Sakurra), 26cr (brgfx), 26bl (bhuvanesb2), 26br (Randy Mets), 27tl (Daniel Eskridge), 27cl (IMG Stock Studio), 27br (MR.AUKID PHUMSIRICHAT), 27bl (Kostyantyn Ivanyshen), 28cl (andychenphoto), 29tr (Richard G Smith), 29cr (Dmitry Demkin); thehistoryblog.com: 9bl; Wikimedia Commons: 7tl (Alexander Roslin, Nationalmuseum, Stockholm, Sweden), 10bl (Robert Hooke, Micrographia, National Library of Wales), 15tl (Maija Karala), 20bl (Charles Darwin and John Gould: The Voyage of the Beagle), 23br (Mendel: Principles of Heredity: A Defence/ Bateson, William).

CONTENTS

Introduction

Science is amazing! It shapes our understanding of the universe and has transformed our everyday lives. At its heart, science is a way of collecting facts, developing ideas to explain those facts, and making predictions we can test.

Laboratory Learning

Chemistry investigates materials, from solids, liquids, and gases to the tiny atoms that make up everything. By understanding the rules behind how different kinds of matter behave, we can create new chemicals and materials with amazing properties.

Scientists can observe chemical reactions under a microscope.

Secrets of the Universe

Physics is the scientific study of energy, forces, mechanics, and waves. Energy includes heat, light, and electricity. Physics also looks at the structure of atoms and the workings of the universe. Even the galaxies obey the laws of physics!

Chimpanzees are one of around 7.8 million species of living animals.

Many forms of energy are involved in a storm.

Life on Earth

Natural history is the study of living things—the countless plants, animals, and other creatures that inhabit Earth now or which existed in the past. It studies how these organisms are influenced by each other and their environment. It also looks at the complex process of evolution—gradual change from one generation to the next.

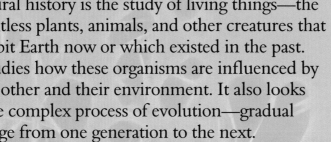

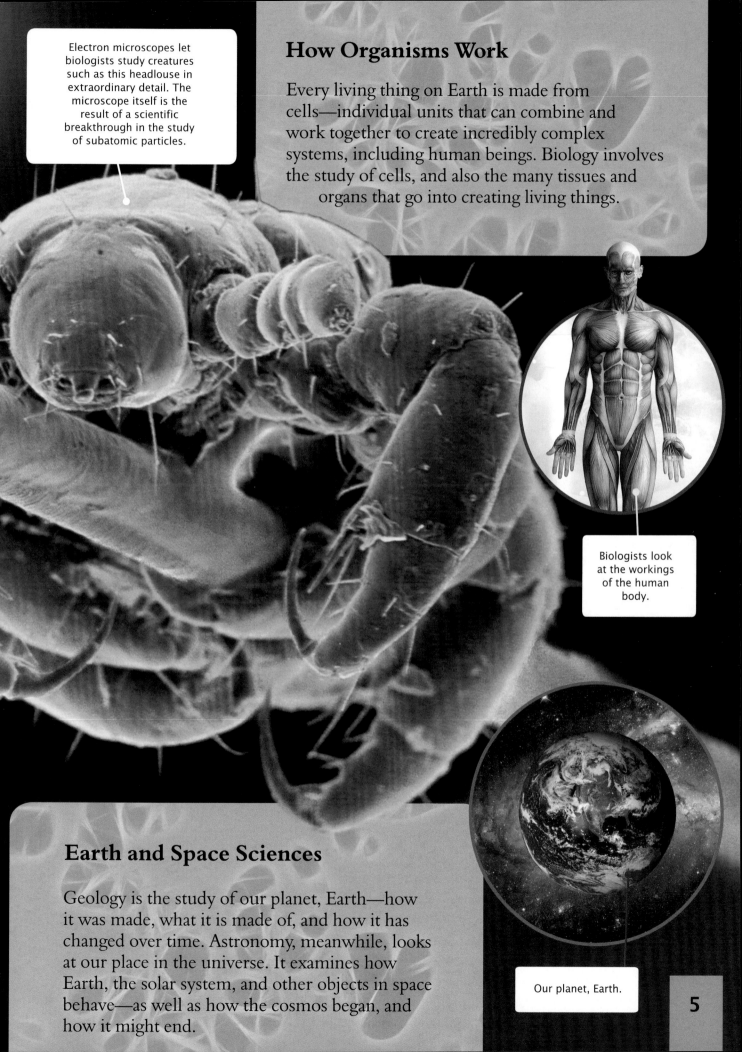

How Organisms Work

Every living thing on Earth is made from cells—individual units that can combine and work together to create incredibly complex systems, including human beings. Biology involves the study of cells, and also the many tissues and organs that go into creating living things.

Biologists look at the workings of the human body.

Earth and Space Sciences

Geology is the study of our planet, Earth—how it was made, what it is made of, and how it has changed over time. Astronomy, meanwhile, looks at our place in the universe. It examines how Earth, the solar system, and other objects in space behave—as well as how the cosmos began, and how it might end.

Our planet, Earth.

Kingdoms of Life

Our planet is home to nearly nine million species (types of living thing). They range from tiny bacteria to blue whales and from humans to giant redwood trees. Biologists group together species that share characteristics to create a complex "tree of life." They organize living things into five kingdoms: animals, plants, fungi, prokaryotes (bacteria and blue-green algae), and protoctists (such as amoebas).

Bacteria use chemical reactions and cell division to survive and copy themselves. The first living organism also did this.

One Big Family

All living things are descended from a single common ancestor—a simple organism that lived about four billion years ago. This organism's descendants found different ways to survive. They branched out to produce the millions of species on Earth today, as well as countless others along the way.

What Is a Species?

Living things belong in the same species if they can breed with each other and produce offspring that can also breed. It's not always possible to test this, but scientists can look for shared genes or body features instead.

Coral reefs, like this one off the island of Fiji in the South Pacific, are home to tens of thousands of species.

Dogs come in an amazing variety of shapes and sizes, but they are a single species. Because their genes are almost identical, different breeds can mate and have puppies.

AMAZING DISCOVERY

Scientist: Carl Linnaeus
Discovery: The tree of life
Date: 1735
The story: Swedish scientist Linnaeus invented a two-name system for classifying every living thing by its genus and species (e.g. *Homo sapiens* for modern humans). This was the first step toward grouping species in a tree of life.

Scientists collect each group of closely related species together into a genus. Related genera are grouped into families, families into orders, orders into classes, classes into phyla, and phyla into kingdoms.

Three-quarters of all living organisms are found on land.

The green sea turtle, *Chelonia mydas*, belongs to a larger family of sea turtles called the Cheloniidae.

Story of DNA

Every living thing has its own set of instructions that tells it how to create the chemicals vital to life—and how to put them together. These instructions, called genes, are found inside a long, twisty molecule called DNA (short for deoxyribonucleic acid).

Pairs and Patterns

The DNA molecule looks like a spiral ladder. The ladder's "rungs" are made of pairs of chemicals called bases. The order of the base pairs spells out a code that can be used to build proteins and other chemicals.

The DNA molecule forms a long, winding ladder shape that is called a double helix.

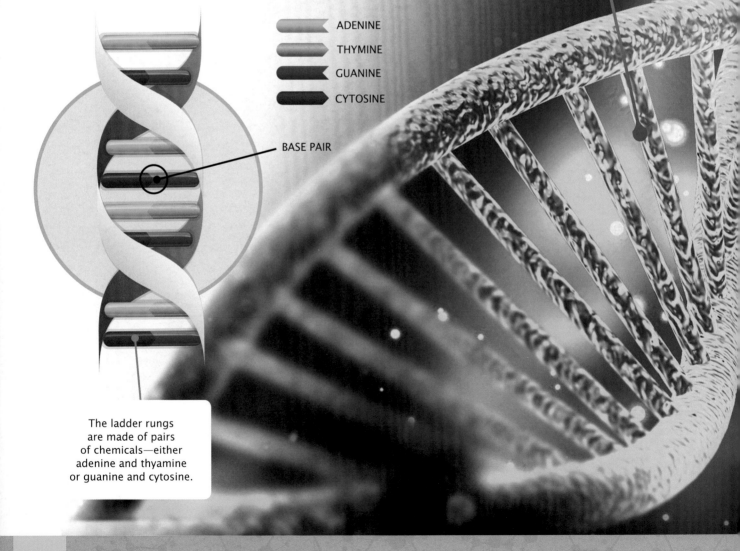

ADENINE

THYMINE

GUANINE

CYTOSINE

BASE PAIR

The ladder rungs are made of pairs of chemicals—either adenine and thyamine or guanine and cytosine.

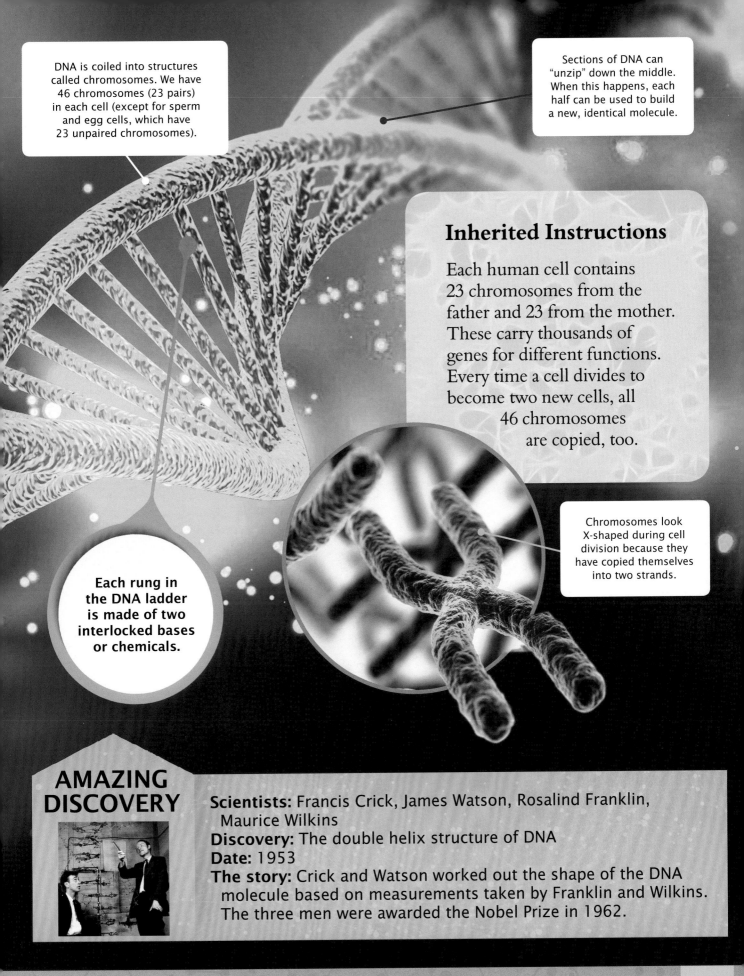

DNA is coiled into structures called chromosomes. We have 46 chromosomes (23 pairs) in each cell (except for sperm and egg cells, which have 23 unpaired chromosomes).

Sections of DNA can "unzip" down the middle. When this happens, each half can be used to build a new, identical molecule.

Inherited Instructions

Each human cell contains 23 chromosomes from the father and 23 from the mother. These carry thousands of genes for different functions. Every time a cell divides to become two new cells, all 46 chromosomes are copied, too.

Chromosomes look X-shaped during cell division because they have copied themselves into two strands.

Each rung in the DNA ladder is made of two interlocked bases or chemicals.

AMAZING DISCOVERY

Scientists: Francis Crick, James Watson, Rosalind Franklin, Maurice Wilkins
Discovery: The double helix structure of DNA
Date: 1953
The story: Crick and Watson worked out the shape of the DNA molecule based on measurements taken by Franklin and Wilkins. The three men were awarded the Nobel Prize in 1962.

Cell Machinery

All living organisms are made up of tiny building blocks called cells. Most cells are microscopic, but they are very complicated. They can convert food into energy, make useful chemicals, and reproduce themselves. The simplest life forms are just one cell; the most complex contain millions.

Two Types of Cell

There are two main types of cell. Bacteria and single-celled organisms have prokaryotic cells—simple cells that do not have a separate nucleus to contain their DNA. Larger organisms have eukaryotic cells. These contain separate chemical machines called organelles that carry out different functions.

ANIMAL CELL ORGANELLES

The golgi store substances for later or get them ready to leave the cell.

Cell membrane

Mitochondrion fuels the cell by releasing energy from sugars, starch, proteins, and fats.

Ribosomes decode DNA and build proteins.

Endoplasmic reticulum makes and stores proteins.

Peroxisome breaks down toxins, proteins, and fatty acids.

Centriole helps the cell divide.

Lyosome breaks down waste.

Prokaryotic cells may have whiplike tails called flagella that help them move around. This *E. coli* bacterium has flagella sticking out in all directions.

AMAZING DISCOVERY

Scientist: Robert Hooke
Discovery: The cell
Date: 1665
The story: English scientist Hooke built some of the first high-powered microscopes. He realized that many body tissues were made up of tiny self-contained units that he named "cells" after the hexagonal structures in honeycomb.

In all eukaryotic cells the nucleus holds most of the genetic material, or DNA.

Making Copies

Cells can reproduce in one of two ways. Mitosis is a process that creates perfect copies. It is used during body growth and to replace damaged or dead cells. Meiosis creates special cells with 23 unpaired chromosomes. The process of meiosis creates our reproductive cells (sperm in males or eggs in females).

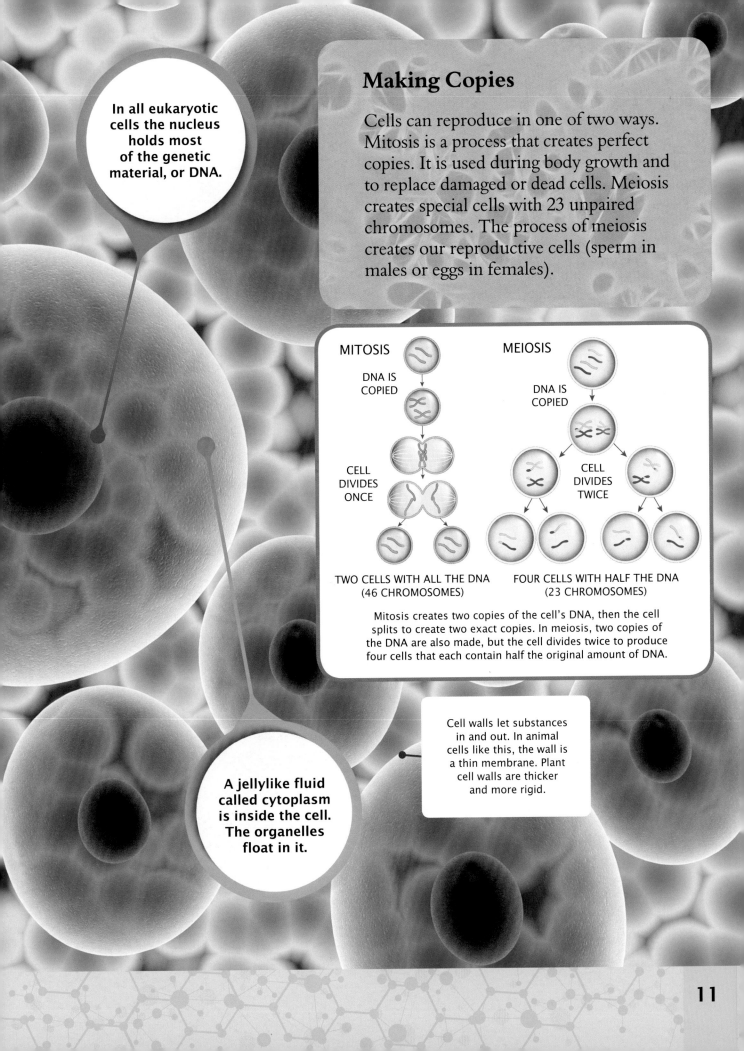

MITOSIS

DNA IS COPIED

CELL DIVIDES ONCE

TWO CELLS WITH ALL THE DNA (46 CHROMOSOMES)

MEIOSIS

DNA IS COPIED

CELL DIVIDES TWICE

FOUR CELLS WITH HALF THE DNA (23 CHROMOSOMES)

Mitosis creates two copies of the cell's DNA, then the cell splits to create two exact copies. In meiosis, two copies of the DNA are also made, but the cell divides twice to produce four cells that each contain half the original amount of DNA.

Cell walls let substances in and out. In animal cells like this, the wall is a thin membrane. Plant cell walls are thicker and more rigid.

A jellylike fluid called cytoplasm is inside the cell. The organelles float in it.

Plants

There are nearly 400,000 plant species on Earth. Plants are living things that can make their own food. During this process they produce oxygen, the gas that all animals, including humans, must breathe to stay alive.

Food from Sunlight

Plants take in carbon dioxide from the air through their leaves and water from the soil through their roots. Then they use the energy in sunlight to transform these ingredients into sugars. This process, called photosynthesis, is a chemical reaction. It takes place in the leaves, helped by a green chemical called chlorophyll.

Sequoia trees can live up to 3,000 years. Some other plants live less than a year.

Plant Reproduction

Seedless plants, such as liverworts, mosses, and ferns, reproduce by releasing spores. If a spore lands in a suitable place, it produces sex cells and, after fertilization, a new plant can grow. Seed plants produce seeds when male sex cells fertilize female ones. A seed contains a complete embryo plant along with a supply of food.

This cross-section of a leaf shows the transportation vessels in the middle. These carry water to the leaf and sugary glucose away from it.

Pollen contains male sex cells. These must reach other flowers to fertilize their female sex cells. Pollen can be carried by insects and birds that visit the flower to feed on nectar.

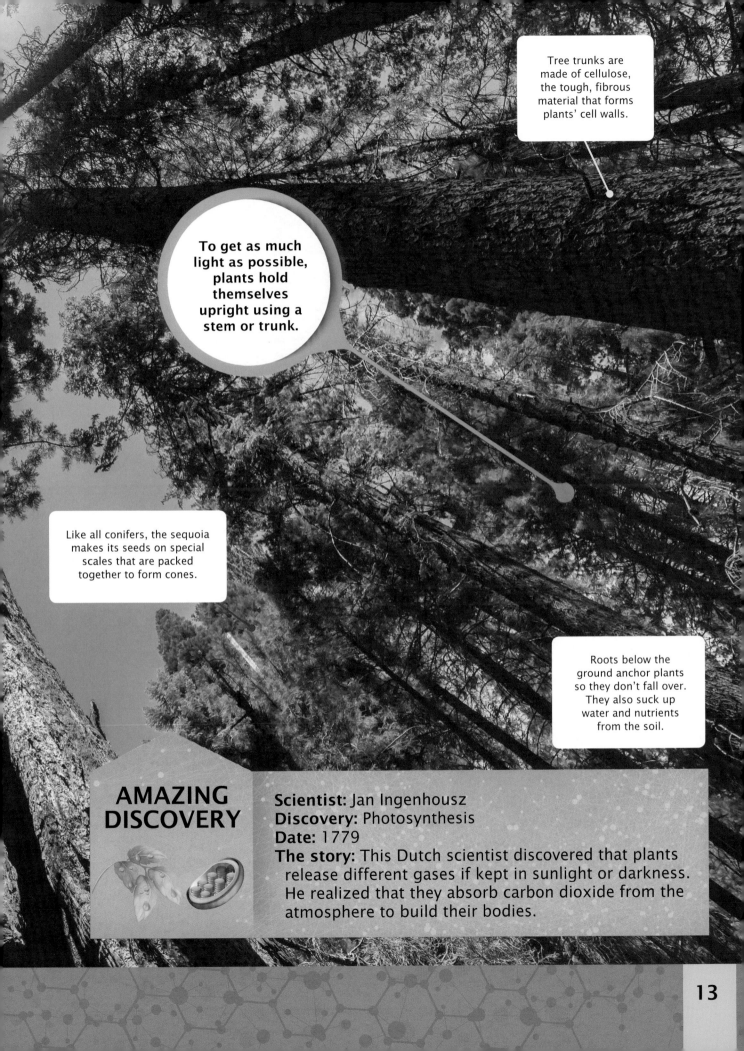

Tree trunks are made of cellulose, the tough, fibrous material that forms plants' cell walls.

To get as much light as possible, plants hold themselves upright using a stem or trunk.

Like all conifers, the sequoia makes its seeds on special scales that are packed together to form cones.

Roots below the ground anchor plants so they don't fall over. They also suck up water and nutrients from the soil.

AMAZING DISCOVERY

Scientist: Jan Ingenhousz
Discovery: Photosynthesis
Date: 1779
The story: This Dutch scientist discovered that plants release different gases if kept in sunlight or darkness. He realized that they absorb carbon dioxide from the atmosphere to build their bodies.

Animals

Animals are living things that get their energy from food, water, oxygen, and the Sun. Unlike plants, they can usually move around in search of food. To harvest energy from their food, animals need to breathe in oxygen.

Animal Types

Fish, amphibians, reptiles, birds, and mammals all have a backbone and skeleton to support their body. They are called vertebrates and make up less than 10 percent of animals. The rest are invertebrates, which don't have a skeleton. They include arthropods, such as insects and spiders, which have a tough outer casing called an exoskeleton, and soft-bodied mollusks.

Symmetry

Most animals have a body plan that is symmetrical—the same on both sides. Features such as limbs and some organs are copied in mirror image. The gut, used to process food, leads from one end of the body to the other.

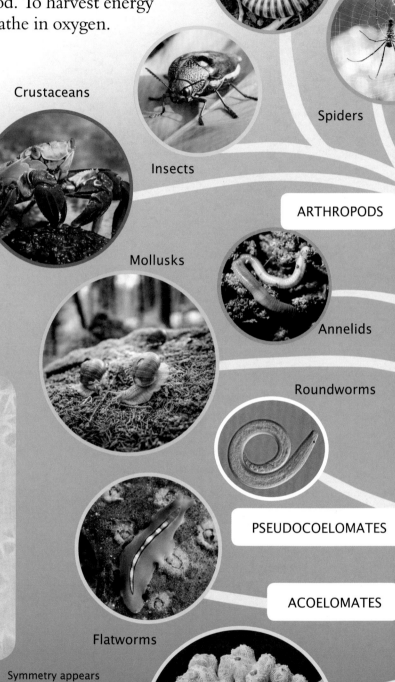

Centipedes and millipedes

Spiders

Crustaceans

Insects

ARTHROPODS

Mollusks

Annelids

Roundworms

PSEUDOCOELOMATES

ACOELOMATES

Flatworms

Symmetry appears in the very first few cells of a developing animal embryo. It often appears in adult features, such as this tiger's beautiful fur.

Sponges

AMAZING DISCOVERY

Scientist: Jennifer Clack
Discovery: *Acanthostega*
Date: 1987
The story: When Clack found a skeleton of *Acanthostega* in Greenland—"Boris"—she realized it was a key step in the evolution of tetrapods (land vertebrates). Boris lived 360 million years ago and had a fishlike body with four legs. She later found tracks of another early tetrapod.

Birds

Reptiles

Mammals

VERTEBRATES

Fish

Amphibians

CHORDATES

PROTOSOMES   DEUTEROSTOMES

Tunicates

COELOMATES

This simple tree shows the different groups in the animal kingdom and how they relate to each other.

RADIATES

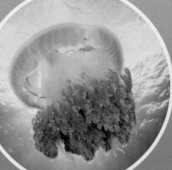

Echinoderms

The huge diversity of animals that exist today all evolved from simple one-celled organisms called protists.

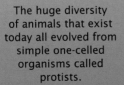

ANCESTRAL PROTISTA

Cnidarians

Web of Life

Living things are connected and dependent on each other through a complex web of relationships known as an ecosystem. These relationships keep the numbers of different species in balance. Species can come under threat if anything upsets this balance, such as changes to the environment.

Everything Is Connected

Plants generate the oxygen that animals need. They are also food for plant-eating animals (herbivores). In turn, meat-eating animals (carnivores) hunt herbivores. All living animals release the carbon dioxide that plants need for photosynthesis. When a plant or animal dies, bacteria, fungi, and other organisms help to recycle its nutrients back into the soil.

The way living things depend on each other for food is called a food chain. A predator, such as a big cat, is right at the top of the food chain because no other animal hunts it.

Plants are called producers because they make their own food. Animals are called consumers because they eat plants and other animals.

Mushrooms are fungi. There are around 5.1 million species of fungus.

AMAZING DISCOVERY

Scientists: James Lovelock, Lynn Margulis
Discovery: Gaia theory
Date: 1972–1979
The story: Chemist Lovelock and microbiologist Margulis showed how living things can affect Earth's atmosphere, oceans, and even rocks. Their Gaia theory argues that our entire planet is a single vast ecosystem.

A tree can be a home to mosses, ivy, and other plants, as well as providing animals with food, oxygen, and shelter.

Most of the fungus is made up of underground threads called hyphae. They feed on nutrients in the soil.

Introduced Species

Within any ecosystem, numbers of different species may go up and down, but they usually return to a balance point. If a new species is introduced into an ecosystem, however, it can have a devastating effect. It competes with the existing species for food, water, space, and breeding sites—and it might also spread disease.

Away from its native Amazon basin and the bugs that feed on it there, the water hyacinth is an invader. It is fast-growing and crowds out other aquatic plants.

Extremes of Life

Most living things need a habitat that offers clean air, a reasonable temperature, and water that is not too acidic or salty. However, some organisms manage to thrive in extreme conditions that would kill most living things.

Coping with Anything

Living things that do well in deadly environments are called extremophiles. Most are single-celled microorganisms. They survive because they have evolved internal chemical processes that stop them being damaged by very high or low temperatures, excess acid or salt, or other difficulties. Many extremophiles can even draw energy from their hostile surroundings.

In the deepest parts of the ocean, volcanic vents pump out scorching, sulfur-rich water. Extremophile microbes survive there and provide the base for an ecosystem that includes deep-sea jellyfish.

Water in Yellowstone Park's hot springs can be 199°F (93°C).

Yellowstone's Grand Prismatic Spring is named for the red, yellow, and green extremophile microbes around its edges.

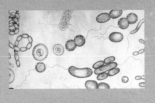

AMAZING DISCOVERY

Scientist: Carl Woese
Discovery: Extreme microbes
Date: 1977
The story: In the mid-1970s, explorers found life thriving in apparently hostile conditions around deep-sea volcanic vents. Woese discovered that these complex ecosystems are based on an entirely new type of single-celled organism, now called archaea.

The orange comes from carotenoids, which the microbes use to carry out photosynthesis.

Hardy Tardigrades

Tardigrades, also known as water bears, are some of the most amazing animals known to science. They usually live among mosses and lichens. However, they can withstand high doses of radiation, extreme hot and cold, dehydration, high pressures, and even exposure to the vacuum of space.

Tardigrades are eight-legged invertebrates probably related to arthropods and velvet worms. They were only discovered in 1773, but have since been found in a huge range of environments.

Darwin's Theory

Why are some species of living thing so similar to each other, and others so different? Does one species change or evolve into another over time? These questions puzzled scientists for centuries—until British naturalist Charles Darwin came up with his theory of evolution by natural selection.

Darwin was inspired by the many new species that explorers were discovering. He also wanted to explain the existence of fossils that were many millions of years old.

Voyage of the *Beagle*

Darwin's theory was driven by his studies aboard the survey ship HMS *Beagle* in the 1830s. In Patagonia he found fossils of giant extinct mammals, such as *Megatherium*. Visiting the isolated Galápagos Islands, Darwin observed finches, marine iguanas, and tortoises that had adapted to different island homes.

Darwin's Finches

There are about 15 finch species across the Galápagos, and they show evolution in action. A single ancestor species became stranded on the volcanic islands some time after their formation. Over time, their descendents spread across the islands and their beaks adapted to suit the main food on each island.

John Gould, the *Beagle*'s natural history artist, sketched the finches in the Galápagos. Their beaks had evolved to suit particular foods. Nut-eaters had large, short bills for cracking shells. Insect-catchers had longer, pointier bills.

This is one of five giant tortoise species on Isabela Island, the most recently formed of the Galápagos Islands.

Each species has a unique shell shape. The tortoises also come in a range of sizes.

Giant tortoises live on seven of the Galápagos Islands. There are more than ten different species.

AMAZING DISCOVERY

Scientists: Charles Darwin (left), Alfred Russel Wallace
Discovery: The origin of species
Date: 1859
The story: Darwin spent 20 years after the *Beagle* developing his ideas about evolution and natural selection. He published his theory only after receiving a letter from Wallace, who had come up with a similar theory while exploring South America and Asia.

Evolution at Work

Evolution explains how living things slowly change over many generations and new species arise. Each individual has a slightly different mix of genetic instructions from its parents. Genes that give it a better chance of survival are more likely to be passed on to the next generation. Over time, individuals with a particular advantage outbreed and replace those without it.

Selection Pressures

Natural selection drives evolution. It's about how individuals adapt to different pressures from the environment. These can include availability of food, competition for mates, threats from predators, diseases, or a changing climate. The fittest usually survive and breed, passing on the genes that helped them cope with the conditions.

Each year, vast herds of wildebeest and zebra migrate across the Serengeti to better grazing. Only the fittest survive.

The journey is tough. It weeds out any individuals that tire easily or are prone to disease.

Megatherium was a giant ground sloth that died out 10,000 years ago. It could not face the selection pressure from changes in its habitat. Today the only sloths are small tree-dwellers.

The most dangerous moment of the migration is when the animals must cross the crocodile-infested Mara river.

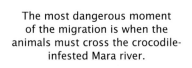

22

Scientist: J. W. Tutt
Discovery: Evolution in the peppered moth
Date: 1896
The story: Tutt suggested that peppered moths had grown darker during the Industrial Revolution. Darker moths were less likely to be spotted and eaten by birds in a polluted, sooty environment, so more of them survived to reproduce.

Crocodiles have evolved to survive for up to a year without food—and then feast.

Evolution and Genes

Although Darwin came up with the theory of evolution, he had no idea how parents passed on adaptations to their offspring. Today we know that evolution works because characteristics are inherited from a mix of both parents' genes, with a little random mutation (due to errors in copying DNA) thrown in.

Austrian monk Gregor Mendel was the first person to identify what we call genes. He noticed them through breeding pea plants with different characteristics. This was in the 1860s, but Mendel's important work was overlooked for decades.

History of Life

Life has existed on Earth for about four billion years. For most of that time, known as the Precambrian, it was just simple, single-celled organisms. From around 540 million years ago (mya), there has been more complex life, and it has passed through distinct phases.

Anomalocaris was an ancestor of arthropods. It lived in the oceans 510 mya, during the Cambrian period.

Divisions of Time

The story of complex life on Earth is usually broken into three stages—the Paleozoic, Mesozoic, and Cenozoic eras (meaning ancient, middle, and recent life). Each era is divided into geological periods lasting tens of millions of years. Geologists identify these periods from the types of rock and the presence of particular fossils.

Fossils of trilobites only come from the six periods that form the Paleozoic. They appeared in the first of these periods, the Cambrian, and went extinct in the last, the Permian.

Mass Extinctions

Throughout history, major changes in life on Earth have begun with natural disasters such as impacts from space, volcanic eruptions, or climate change. These disasters wipe out many of the previously dominant animals, leaving the way open for new ones to take their place.

About 65 mya, the effects of a huge asteroid impact drove the dinosaurs to extinction. Since then, mammals have become the main large land animals.

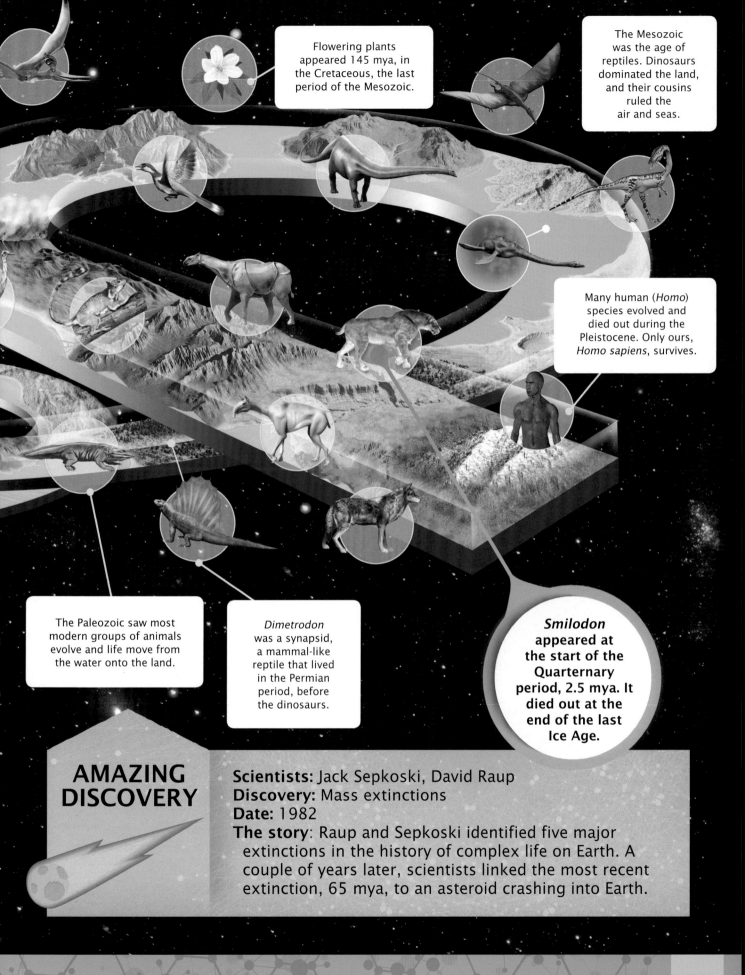

Flowering plants appeared 145 mya, in the Cretaceous, the last period of the Mesozoic.

The Mesozoic was the age of reptiles. Dinosaurs dominated the land, and their cousins ruled the air and seas.

Many human (*Homo*) species evolved and died out during the Pleistocene. Only ours, *Homo sapiens*, survives.

The Paleozoic saw most modern groups of animals evolve and life move from the water onto the land.

Dimetrodon was a synapsid, a mammal-like reptile that lived in the Permian period, before the dinosaurs.

Smilodon appeared at the start of the Quarternary period, 2.5 mya. It died out at the end of the last Ice Age.

AMAZING DISCOVERY

Scientists: Jack Sepkoski, David Raup
Discovery: Mass extinctions
Date: 1982
The story: Raup and Sepkoski identified five major extinctions in the history of complex life on Earth. A couple of years later, scientists linked the most recent extinction, 65 mya, to an asteroid crashing into Earth.

Fun Facts

Now that you have discovered lots about life on Earth, boost your knowledge further with these 10 quick facts!

Scientists estimate that about 99 percent of all the species that have ever lived are now extinct.

The longest human chromosome, known as chromosome 1, contains more than 249 million base pairs.

Animal cells are usually between 0.00004 in (0.001 mm) and 0.004 in (0.1 mm) in size.

Some plants grow at amazing speeds. Bamboo can shoot up by as much as 35 in (91 cm) in a single day.

Arthropods account for 80 percent of all known animal species. Most are small, but the Japanese spider crab has a legspan up to 18 ft (5.5 m).

The dodo, a giant flightless bird from Mauritius, died out within 80 years of humans and their rats, pigs, dogs, and cats landing on its island home.

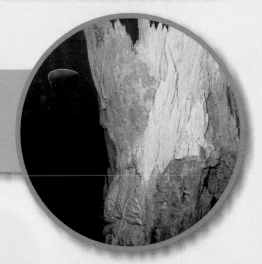

Life may have evolved around deep-sea vents before adapting to other conditions. If so, land-living animals and plants are the real extremophiles!

French scientist Jean-Baptiste Lamarck was the first to suggest species arise through a process of evolution in 1800—but he couldn't explain how.

Biologists study evolution at high speed using the Drosophila fruit fly—a species that can produce a new generation every ten days!

Birds evolved from dinosaurs called theropods. They survived the mass extinction 65 mya, but the other dinosaurs did not.

Your Questions Answered

We know an incredible amount about how life on Earth began and evolved into today's rich diversity. But there is always more to discover. Scientists are still identifying new species, carrying out in-depth research into genetics, and continuing to find out more incredible details about our ecosystem. This new knowledge can help us understand our world better and keep us inquisitive about our environment. Here are some questions that can help you understand even more about this vast and fascinating topic.

Which animal and plant species have survived the longest?

In evolutionary history, most species on our planet have gradually developed new features, adapted to their environment in different ways, and thus changed significantly over time. But there are a few exceptions in the plant and animal world, with species surviving for hundreds of millions of years, almost unchanged. These include animals such as the nautilus, which has survived for over 500 million years, and plants such as ferns, which were growing on our planet over 350 million years ago.

Jellyfish are the oldest multi-organ animals, having already been on Earth 600–700 million years ago!

What is gene mutation?

Every time a cell divides, whether during mitosis or meiosis, there is a possibility of a mistake occurring while the genetic material is being copied. This slight change remains, and is passed on during each following cell division. It is called a mutation, and, essentially, it introduces variation within a species. Mutations are essential to evolution—those that result in useful features may mean that affected individuals are better able to survive, passing this new feature on to their offspring.

What is the oldest living organism?

Of all organisms on our planet, trees are those that can live the longest by far. It isn't unusual for a chestnut tree to survive for 200 or 300 years. However, by far the oldest living organism is a bristlecone pine tree in California, which is over 5,060 years old. It was already present when the ancient Egyptians started building pyramids!

Bristlecone pine trees are native to the Rocky Mountains; it is not unusual for them to survive for more than 1,000 years.

Are there any animals that have an asymmetrical body plan?

Most animals appear symmetrical (on the outside). However, there are some animals that show a degree of asymmetry, for example fiddler crabs, who have two claws, one on each side of their body, but one is significantly larger than the other. Another example is the flat fish, whereby both eyes are on one side of the body. But these animals all start their development with a symmetrical body that later develops the asymmetries. The one animal that is completely asymmetrical from its earliest development stages is the sponge. It is made of a mass of single cells that grow together in no particular pattern and start acting as one organism.

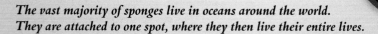

The vast majority of sponges live in oceans around the world. They are attached to one spot, where they then live their entire lives.

Which introduced species has caused the most devastation?

When a species is introduced to a new ecosystem this often has serious consequences. The new "invasive" species disturbs the balance of the habitat's creatures and plants, which can lead to devastating effects. It is hard to estimate which introduced species has caused the most harm to its new ecosystem, but one famous example is the cane toad in Australia. In 1935, 3,000 toads were imported as a pest control. However, they did not prove helpful in controlling the pest, and instead became one themselves! They multiplied incredibly quickly and their toxic skin has killed a huge amount of local wildlife. Today, there are over 200 million cane toads in Australia and some native species are close to extinction.

Glossary

chromosome A thread-like structure of DNA. It is found in the nucleus of most living cells and carries the genetic information.

DNA Short for deoxyribonucleic acid, the chemical ingredient that forms genes. Parents pass on copied parts of their DNA to their children so that some of their traits (such as height and hair type) are also passed on.

eukaryotic cell A cell that holds the genetic information as DNA in chromosomes. The chromosomes are housed in a nucleus.

evolution The process by which species develop and change with each new generation, in order to better suit their environment and increase their chances of survival.

extinction When all members of a species, or family, are no longer alive.

extremophile A creature that thrives in conditions that are too extreme for other species to survive in.

fungi Small organisms that form part of a larger group including yeasts and mushrooms.

gene A combination of chemicals that carries information about how an organism will appear.

meiosis A type of cell division that results in four daughter cells, each with half the set of the chromosomes of the parent cell.

mitosis A type of cell division that results in each of the two daughter cells having the same amount of chromosomes as the parent cell.

molecule A group of atoms bonded together to form what is known as a chemical compound. A molecule is the smallest particle that still has all of the chemical properties of a substance.

prokaryotic cell A cell that doesn't have a nucleus or any other cell organelles. Bacteria often consist of one prokaryotic cell.

protein One of the most important of all molecules in the body, protein is needed to strengthen and replace tissue in the body. Muscles and many organs are made of protein.

species A group of living beings that is able to breed with each other and produce offspring that can also breed.

Further Information

BOOKS

Claybourne, Anna. *Mind Webs: Living Things.* London, UK: Wayland Books, 2015.

DK Publishing. *Knowledge Encyclopedia: Animal!* London, UK: DK Children, 2016.

Ignotofsky, Rachel. *Women In Science: 50 Fearless Pioneers Who Changed The World.* London, UK: Wren and Rook, 2017.

Richards, Jon, and Ed Simkins. *Science In Infographics: Living Things.* London, UK: Wayland Books, 2017.

Winston, Robert: *Big Questions: All About Biology.* London, UK: DK Children, 2016.

WEBSITES

Bitesize Biology
https://www.bbc.com/education/examspecs/zpgcbk7
Explore this BBC webpage and find out much more about life on our planet.

NECSI Activities
http://www.necsi.edu/projects/evolution/activities/intro./activities_intro.html
Head to this website for fun activities that help you explore evolution.

Plants and Animals on Earth
http://www.thunderboltkids.co.za/Grade5/01-life-and-living/chapter1.html
Discover activities that investigate animals and plants in their ecosystems.

Index

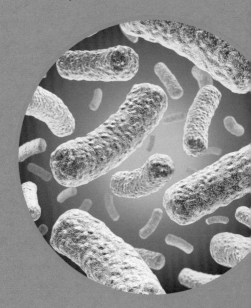